BEFORE THEM ALL

A GREEN FIG BOOK

Illustrated & Designed by

CHY Illustration & Design

God does not have a beginning
Everythig else has a beginning

Name:

_____

Note to Parents & Educators

The Prophet, may peace be upon him, said: "God existed and nothing else existed." This means God existed and there was no earth, no skies, no place, no time, no darkness or light, nor anything of the universe. God existed before He created all these things. God has no beginning. God is eternal.

The Qur'anic texts and the mental proofs necessitate that the Creator of the universe has to be eternal. Had God not been eternal, He would have a beginning. This necessitates that He would be in need of someone to give him a beginning, and the one in need is not God. It is impossible for the Creator to be created, that is, to come into existence from non-existence. God's existence is not preceded by non-existence.

Before Them All is a book about the Eternality of God. The concept is presented to children in short rhyming sentences and beautiful watercolor illustrations.

We like to hear from you and your children at info@gogreenfig.com

Green Fig Staff

God existed

Before the birds and the trees

Before the fish and the seas

Before the mountains and the plains

Before the wind and the rains

I Love Angels

Before the angels in the skies

Before the colored butterflies

Before the animals roamed around

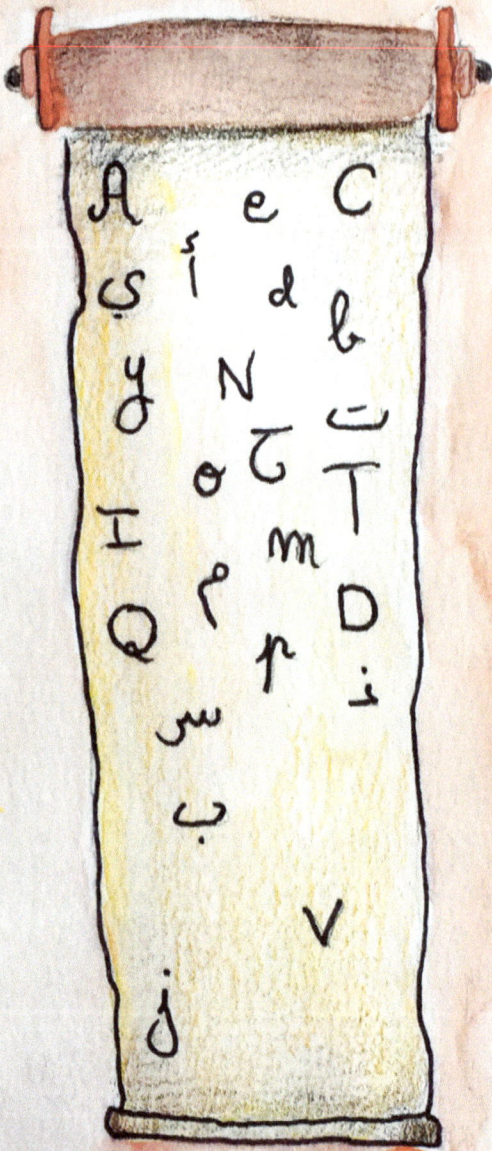

Before the letters and the sound

Before you and me

God existed eternally

Before the moon and the sun

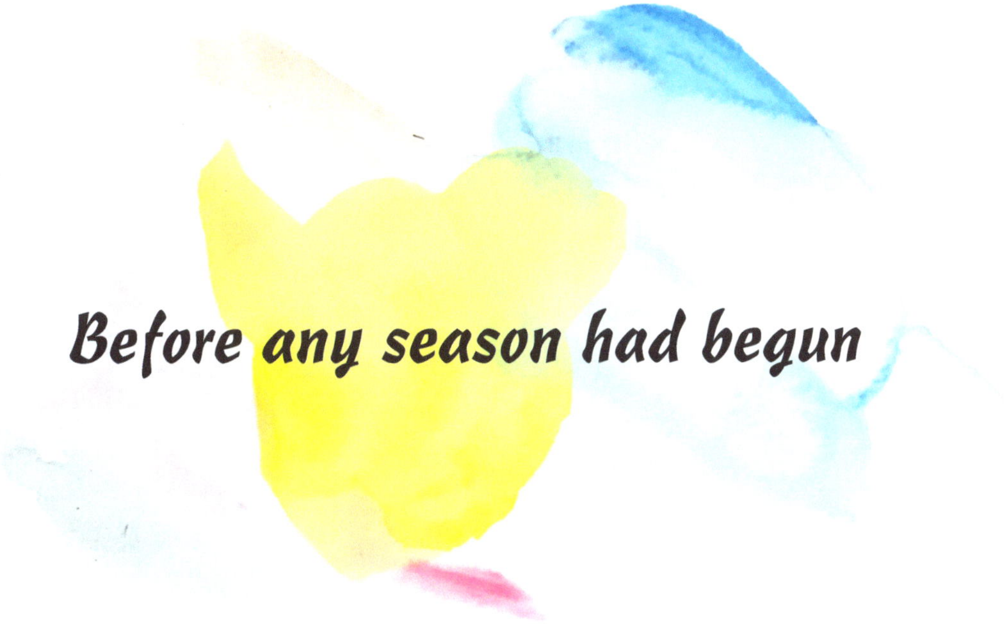

Before any season had begun

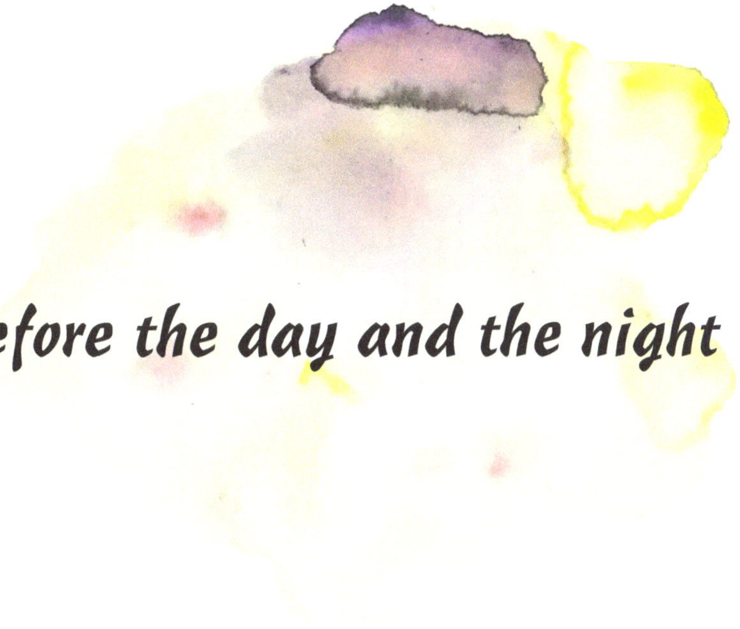

Before the day and the night

Before the darkness and the light

2:38

Before the time and the place

Before the stars twinkled in space

Before the heavens and the earths

Before all of the universe

God existed eternally

God existed before He created all these things

God existed before everything!

God always existed

God existed eternally.

Encourage your child to memorize:

God said in Surat al-Hadid verse 3#:

﴿هُوَ الْأَوَّلُ﴾

Which means:
"God is the only One without a beginning."

The Prophet, may peace be upon him, said:

كان اللَّه ولم يَكُنْ شَىءٌ غَيْرُهُ

Which means:
"God existed eternally and nothing else existed."
Narrated by al-Bukhariyy

The Proud Muslim Kids series by Green Fig is designed to engagingly teach youngsters basic concepts of Islam in a way that speaks to their hearts and minds. Each book in the series is crafted by a staff of qualified educators, writers, illustrators, parents and children. Not only is the Proud Muslim Kids series designed to supplement the early childhood and elementary Islamic curriculum, it is a great addition to any school or home library. Covering a wide variety of topics such as the Five Pillars of Islam, Islamic culture, and Islamic history, parents and children will return to these books and enjoy them together time and time again.

Green Fig

www.ingramcontent.com/pod-product-compliance
Lightning Source LLC
Chambersburg PA
CBHW041547040426
42447CB00002B/80